# Dysfunctional:

## Can we learn to get along?

**PENELOPE D.**

CAN'T WE LEARN TO GET ALONG?

# DYSFUNCTIONAL

Copyright © 2015 Penelope Davis

All rights reserved. No part of this book may be reproduced or transmitted in any form or by any means, electronic or mechanical, including photocopying, recording, or by any information storage and retrieval system, without permission in writing from the publisher. All questions and/or request are to be submitted to: 134 Andrew Drive, Reidsville NC, 27320.

To the best of said publisher knowledge, this is an original manuscript and is the sole property of author **PENELOPE DAVIS**

Printed in the United States of America

**ISBN-13:978-0692607299**
**ISBN-10:0692607293**

Printed by Createspace 2015
Published by BlaqRayn Publishing Plus 2015

DYSFUNCTIONAL

# DEDICATION

Dysfunctional is dedicated to all of you who come from dysfunctional families or are affected in some way by dysfunctional people in your lives. It's really a problem. We don't look it at as a problem because we've accepted for so many years that being dysfunctional is normal. It's not normal and if you or anyone you know are not functioning properly,

Get Help!!!

CAN'T WE LEARN TO GET ALONG?

# Dysfunctional:

# Can we learn to get along?

**PENELOPE D.**

## DYSFUNCTIONAL

If ever you were told that you are dysfunctional, or you come from a dysfunctional family, chances are the person that told you that was probably on to something. If there are any malfunctions, in any area of your life, meaning relationships, friendships, behaviors, or conflicts; you are dysfunctional. Your mama, your daddy, your grandparents, uncles, aunts, and cousins. Your whole family is dysfunctional, I know mine is...

A lot of us come from large families and sometimes it works, but the majority of the time, you will find that we don't always like our families, or certain family members.

## CAN'T WE LEARN TO GET ALONG?

Either because one sets himself/herself on a high pedestal and looks down on other family members, or the parents show favoritism, at least it seems that way. There could be reasons far in between, but it's not normal.

We have accepted different types of malfunctions as normal because that's all we know, especially black families. We don't operate properly, we deviate from the norms of social behavior, in every way imaginable. There is always conflict or misbehavior of some kind. Your parents and her siblings aren't speaking for whatever reason, then there is a barrier between you and your cousins, y'all can't talk, because your parents

## DYSFUNCTIONAL

don't talk, and you don't even know why. Fortunately enough, my cousins and I still talk and we're close. We may have our disagreements at times but we are extremely close, and being one of the oldest of many, I've always made sure my younger cousins were okay.

Some won't show up to family events because they don't want to see the one who pissed them off last year, but it is what it is, and It's all bullshit to me. We all have the mindset that blood is thicker than water, but often times we would say that we are closer to our good friends than we are to our own family.

## CAN'T WE LEARN TO GET ALONG?

**What a contradiction!**

Your friends may be around you more; that may be because the unity that's supposed to exist among family doesn't exist at all. Get into an altercation, that requires back up, then watch how quickly your friends run. I bet you'll see how close y'all really are then.

I hear all the time, "I don't like so, and so" or "she and her kids think they are better than everyone else"; people are saying these things about their own family members.

**But why? So glad you asked!**

## DYSFUNCTIONAL

Because that's what our parents/grandparents taught us and we have grown up with ill feelings, hatred towards our own families. We compete, talk bad about each other, hold grudges for no apparent reason, make it known to people outside of family that we don't like one another and then wonder why they look at us funny. The sad part is, most of the time, we don't even know why we're so disgusted with our families...we need to do better because at the end of the day, we can't change DNA and family *is* really all we have.

I knew things weren't right in my family the moment when most parents would say "get my belt" but my grandfather said instead,

## CAN'T WE LEARN TO GET ALONG?

"get my gun"! Most kids got beatings/spankings, and, because I was abused early on in life, I'm not a fan of physical discipline; however, I think I'd prefer being popped any day, to being chased with a loaded gun.

Of course, my grandfather never shot or even aimed a gun at his kids or grand kids but for him to ask for it, instead of a belt, and for us to laugh, as if it were normal, was definitely dysfunctional. I love my family, even at crazy times, when we don't see eye to eye, or just don't talk to each other for whatever reason, family is family, and when it's time to come together, we do just that. I only wish we

## DYSFUNCTIONAL

could all get along. My grandparents had ten kids, 7 girls and 3 boys, and with so many women, conflict is expected just not justified.

Now black women, we are the epitome of dysfunctional. There is so much hatred and envy among us, it is utterly ridiculous. All the nice clothes, hair, make up, beautiful homes, and fancy cars in the world will not make us function properly. I hear the plus size women saying all the time how much they hate skinny bitches.

**But why?**

## CAN'T WE LEARN TO GET ALONG?

If you want to be skinny or smaller, do what you have to do and stop making excuses as to why you're as heavy as you are, the skinny bitch didn't put the extra pounds on you, **YOU DID!** I've been small all of my life, never over a size 3. People have even accused me of being on drugs because I was so small but I was never mad at those who were bigger, who cares? I get that for some, it's your genetic make up, or health issues that may cause you to be bigger than you would like to be,some small women have health issues which causes them to be small, nothing gives you the right to be so mad at the smaller women. Embrace your full figured curves, live your life, and be happy.

## DYSFUNCTIONAL

The same goes for small women, we throw shade at the big girls all the time, and we don't know their story. Just mad because they have more curves and the men give them more attention, so you think, or because their clothes fit them better. Go sit down somewhere and eat. Get you a couple of Twinkies and just eat. Your metabolism too high? Well slow it down and have a couple of biscuits or just be happy with yourself and leave the big girls alone.

We torture each other because of our own deep issues. We hide behind the make up, fake lashes, clothes, shoes, jewelry; we appear to be happy and to have it going on.

## CAN'T WE LEARN TO GET ALONG?

Some of us do, but at the end of the day, when you're driving your fancy car, you pull into the driveway of your beautiful home, you go inside and began to unwind from a hectic day on your successful job and as you began to take off all the layers of make up (some of us pile it on thick) and your bomb outfit, you look in the mirror, becoming disgusted. You're disgusted, not because you're ugly, (I think we all are beautiful), because at that moment, you realize how dysfunctional you really are. You see the **REAL YOU!** The lonely, miserable you that no one knows, the messy you who lives to stir up trouble, the simple you who doesn't speak to "Sally",

## DYSFUNCTIONAL

because your BFF doesn't speak to her (followers).

The nasty you that sleeps with everybody's man because your self esteem is too low for you to even attempt to get your own, or, you need your bills paid and can't pay them yourself. You see the person that hates for anyone to have anything more than you have, the pretender.

You aren't happy at all your friend just got that promotion, a raise, or that she's newly engaged. You're mad because you want the life your friend has. You're nobody's friend for real, you really don't know how to be a

## CAN'T WE LEARN TO GET ALONG?

real genuine friend because you're not genuine with yourself.

**You're fake!**

Fake just like the lashes you wear. You're not loyal at all, only to your need for people, and once your needs change or get met, your loyalties change. You don't even know what it means to be loyal. Just because you look out for a person doesn't make you loyal, sit down somewhere! People have looked out for you, but what does that mean to you?

You may have people in your life that you've known forever, that's excellent, but you're not

## DYSFUNCTIONAL

a loyal friend in any way. You will talk about your so called dear ones and sell their souls to the devil if the price is right. In that mirror, you see the hater that you are; how envious you really are of your friends. You see the person that will go to the extreme for attention, even if it means making a mockery of your true friends; the ones that accept you flaws and all.

The ride or die chick your homies think you are...they better think again because you're not. You ride or die when things are good or when it's beneficial to you but when it's time to show and prove, you find every reason to

## CAN'T WE LEARN TO GET ALONG?

not be around; you're all of sudden riding solo.

**You are a dysfunctional soul!**

Reason being, you don't have one ounce of love for yourself. You feed off making everyone around you as miserable as you are, but you will not steal my joy. I won't allow it!

If we could first learn to love ourselves as women, appreciate who we are, accept our own flaws, do what needs to be done to fix them and embrace the skin we're in, we could love each other as we should. Can't we learn

## DYSFUNCTIONAL

to get along? Whatever happened to "I am my sister's keeper"?

I'm in no way saying that all women are the same. There are some women who are genuine, down to earth people and will ride with you til the end, but so many are not. If we could all pull together, as black women, we would be so powerful, even Superman could not tear us apart. We wouldn't have to hide behind material things. If you are successful, give your girl, your sister a hand, share with her what you did to become successful. Help her find what it is she wants to do in order to have her own success story. Don't look down on her or belittle her in any

## CAN'T WE LEARN TO GET ALONG?

way. It's rude as hell and she's probably already down, being hard enough on herself. Speak kind words of encouragement to her, and let her know that you're there for her, that she to can be just as successful. She may not be as motivated as she'd like to be and just needs a little push.

You can't go around flaunting in your **friends'** faces how successful you are, that's not cool. They are the ones who watched you come from nothing, probably helping you along the way. Success speaks for itself. It's okay to be proud of your accomplishments, you deserve to be proud. Success takes hard work and dedication, but remain humble, and

## DYSFUNCTIONAL

be mindful of how you treat people. You never know when you may need someone or who will be there for you. God blessed you to be a blessing to others. Never walk around thinking you're better than the next, you're not! You've only made better choices and your choices are what sets you apart from others. In no way are you better than anyone else. Your shit stinks and you still have to put your pants on one leg at a time; if you're putting them on differently, then It's **you** with the problem. You are dysfunctional as hell!

I get that you are not as successful as you would like to be, but it doesn't make it right for you to be so mad and hate on those who

## CAN'T WE LEARN TO GET ALONG?

are. You determine your own success and your destiny in life. You have to decide for yourself the kind of life you want to live. If you want average then just be almost successful, and don't be so bothered by those who live a lavish lifestyle. If you want to live well above average, then do what you have to do to make things happen for yourself. Make everyone proud, but most of all, make yourself proud and happy.

There is room at the top for us all. I think if we all learned to get along, to give each other a helping hand, the black community would be okay. So many other races/communities see how bad we treat each other, think it's

## DYSFUNCTIONAL

okay to mistreat us, and we can't be mad because we teach them through our own actions.

What really bothers me the most is we treat each other badly in an attempt to impress others, when in all actuality, they think we are stupid for the way we behave. They look at us, and shake their heads in shame; they would never mistreat their own to impress or gain attention from us. They aren't impressed in any way. In fact, they think of us as less than human when we treat each other so badly. It's not okay at all, and the only way to make them understand that it's not okay, would be to do the unimaginable, and come

## CAN'T WE LEARN TO GET ALONG?

together. It's unexpected for us to come together as a community. However, it is expected for us to continue to hate each other, fight/kill each other, steal from each other, hurt each other's kids, be envious of one another and send each other to jail.

Other communities, along with society as a whole, look forward to it all; it makes their job easier. Now if we were to change the game a bit, join forces with each other, gave each other a lift up, and even grabbed their hands along the way, they would have no choice, but to go with the flow. I say we start with each other, especially us women. No

## DYSFUNCTIONAL

one can handle black women standing strong, and coming together, that's gangsta!

Wouldn't you love to see the day when we all could sit, laugh, talk and break bread with each other without any conflict or drama? It would be so sweet! Ladies we are some bad bitches, we are smart as hell, for the most part independent, and not ever scared to get those coins. We work just as hard, if not harder than most men, and still manage to take care of home, the kids, and look good doing it all.

Instead of living like crabs in a bucket, pulling each other down, reach down and pull each other to the top. What reason do we

## CAN'T WE LEARN TO GET ALONG?

have to let each other fall? Some of us may not be mature enough just yet, to help other communities, although we should because God created us all, but we're all a work in progress, and they're not in any way trying to help us. Other communities are intimidated by us, afraid of what we'll become as a whole, but we're to blind to see that.

Men are not exempt from being dysfunctional either. They have jealousy among themselves as well. They shoot and kill each other over some of the simplest things, such as: "the home boy slept with my girl." Doesn't that mean your girl was involved? It also means she was unfaithful,

## DYSFUNCTIONAL

so are you gonna kill or go after every guy she sleeps with? If she did it once, she'll do it again but instead of just leaving her alone, you go on a killing spree? What type of sense does that make? How about getting off your girl's couch in the living room of her Section 8 apartment, get a job and help her to do better. Or, concentrate on being a father/positive role model to your kids and supporting them financially, without being forced to do so. You complain that we put y'all on paper, but won't do what is necessary to prevent us from doing so. We don't like having to bring our black men to shame, making it hard for them to get ahead because

## CAN'T WE LEARN TO GET ALONG?

you owe child support, but you leave us no choice.

Stop creating families that you have no intentions on being a part of, then get upset when Child Support Enforcement gets involved. I know a lot of women use child support as a threat to keep men around, but what about the ones who just need you to be responsible, what are we supposed to do? We should never have to ask you to take care of your children, they are people just like we are and everything you need to survive daily, your kids need as well. Y'all don't have to ask us to take care of them, so why do you sit

## DYSFUNCTIONAL

around waiting on us to ask you to do the same?

I know sometimes men raise kids on their own and my hat goes off to you...welcome to our world...

**It's hard isn't it?**

Raising kids is a hard enough job in itself. Instead of you complaining about how your kids are being raised because it's not to your liking, appreciate your kids' mother for holding it down in your absence. Don't be upset once she has moved on and her new man has taken your place. That same man has

## CAN'T WE LEARN TO GET ALONG?

stepped up to the plate, taking on the role of being 'daddy" to your kids, you ought to shake that man's hand.

Some of you are happy that you're no longer responsible, that someone else has taken over and assumed responsibility for your kids, but the sad part is, the minute your kids become successful or make it big, you expect some type of recognition for being his/her father; that's not cool. You make the **REAL MEN** look bad when you choose not to function properly. Your behavior plays a part in how these kids choose to live their own lives as adults. I know some of you take excellent care of your kids, you're actively involved

## DYSFUNCTIONAL

and your kids' mothers still make you pay child support. Please don't let that trifling heifer determine how you look at the rest of us.

Ladies don't say "AMEN" just yet. We chose our kids' fathers and they showed us who they really were from the start, we just ignored the obvious thinking they would change...joke is on us! You can't complain when you knew from the start he wasn't shit. It was confirmed when he moved in and couldn't help you pay your $50.00 a month rent but you let him stay anyway because you love his funky ass boxers....girl sit down!

## CAN'T WE LEARN TO GET ALONG?

It's all good though. We all are gonna be just fine. I guess we all have to first recognize how dysfunctional we really are within ourselves so we can become better individuals. Know and understand we all come with flaws but it's okay. No one is perfect. You have to make a conscious decision to strive for perfection or at least be better than what you used to be. Accept you will never be perfect, put forth the effort and realize your only competition should be yourself.

A lot of times, we shift the blame on other people for our mistakes; no one is to blame, other than ourselves. So what if your parents

## DYSFUNCTIONAL

weren't there for you when you were a kid, it doesn't justify you being a loser. My parents didn't raise or take care of me at all, but I was/am determined to be great; being a loser has never an option. I'm not flawless, I have imperfections, but I've accepted that my flaws are a part of who I am and to deal with me, means to accept me flaws and all. If you can't , then you should move on.

Dysfunctional relationships make normal relationships look bad because we're so accepting of what is not supposed to be. You can never say that you're in a healthy, happy relationship if you give your partner so much control, you think it's unreal for you to have a

## CAN'T WE LEARN TO GET ALONG?

mind of your own. You don't think for yourself, you don't voice your own opinions, you don't wear certain clothing because your partner says you can't. Your jeans have to be 3 sizes too big and you can only wear your hair a certain way. Hell, some will even go as far as to change religions. This is crazy as hell; you may as well be a robot. That's some dysfunctional shit.

I have already accepted that I just may be by myself forever; I'm okay with that. I just don't see giving a man that much control over me. I'm gonna wear what the hell I want to wear, and that's just it. My hair has grown out of my own damn scalp and I will do what I want

## DYSFUNCTIONAL

with it. I'm definitely gonna say what I want to say and no one is gonna stop me...**NO ONE!** Yes, I curse, so what! Do what pleases your mate....boy bye!

Some men expect us to bow down to them, as if we're servants or something. That's not why we were created. We were created from your rib, the bones that protect your heart and lungs. Not from your feet, to be under you; nor from your head to be above you, but from your side, to stand beside you and hold close to you. When you mistreat us, you're only damaging your own heart. Besides, what about what pleases me?

## CAN'T WE LEARN TO GET ALONG?

Living in the flesh, I sometimes unintentionally have a hard time being obedient to **GOD**, I know damn well I can't be that obedient to a man, because he thinks I should be. Lol, that's real funny, y'all got me messed up! I am my own individual, and I have a mind of my own. I may respect you as a man, but I can't change who I am. I don't know how to be anyone else, and besides, that would make me fake wouldn't it? I like being true to who I am, and you should as well. Never change or apologize for who you are. I hear both men and women saying they aren't allowed to do certain things, or go certain places or be around certain people because their significant other said so, that's

## DYSFUNCTIONAL

bullshit. If they don't trust you enough to know you have enough respect for **YOURSELF** (not even about them) and that you will conduct yourself in a respectful manner, wherever you are, whomever you're with, then they are having their own insecurity issues. What, where, when, who, and how shouldn't even matter. I'm not doing any explaining, I don't feel like it, and I'm not about to ask any questions. Respect me and I'll respect you. Carry yourself like you have good damn sense, and I'll do the same. Anything else is drama, and I don't need it. You're not my daddy and you're lucky that I let you be my man.

## CAN'T WE LEARN TO GET ALONG?

Women are insecure as well; you won't let your man be a man. He can't hang out with his boys, have a beer or even go to the barber shop without you complaining. And yes, sometimes they bring it on themselves because they were dishonest a time or two, but we have to learn to let it go or let them go; eventually they'll leave anyway. When he starts saying he's not happy and wants to be single, you better pay attention, he's definitely on his way out. Rather it be next week, next month, next year or the next 3 years, he's leaving, so get ready. If he doesn't leave, prepare yourself to be "the other woman"; eventually, that's what you'll be. It doesn't matter if you share the same last name

## DYSFUNCTIONAL

and address, if he's not happy you are no longer a priority, his happiness is. So don't think for one second that because he decided to stay, y'all are working things out. He's just finding what he thinks is happiness with someone else. It's cheaper to keep you around and it doesn't matter how dysfunctional your home is. If your man is sleeping in another room and is not bothered by it, he is done with you. There is absolutely no way you can honestly say you're happy living that kind of life.

Maybe you can say it to fool other people on the outside but you can't fool yourself. I'm no expert on marriage or relationships, but I was

## CAN'T WE LEARN TO GET ALONG?

married for 18 years. My marriage was dysfunctional as hell, damn near invited dysfunction, and I know now what's real. All it takes is common sense.

Not all marriages and/or relationships are dysfunctional, some are really strong unions, that work. It's a beautiful thing when it's right and two people are together for all the right reasons. So many people now marry for convenience, benefits, security or what a person can do for them. It's not genuine anymore.

Even in relationships, people get involved just to say they have someone or just for sex.

## DYSFUNCTIONAL

Most of the time, there isn't any intention on longevity, just until you find "**the one**". No one has time for all that foolishness. If we're not dating with a purpose and you can't incorporate me in your future plans, as the **Mrs.** then we really shouldn't be dating. I just think if you're often having to guess what your role is in a person's life, then you really don't have a role. If your significant other tells you that he/she doesn't know where you're headed or what exactly it is you're doing, you probably aren't doing anything. it's about sex, nothing more, so don't get your hopes up. Anyone can feed you, buy you nice things, make small talk and sleep with you, but if they're not interested in making you a

## CAN'T WE LEARN TO GET ALONG?

better you and riding with you til the end, move on because you're just the temp service. They don't want you for real, you're just something to do in order to kill time. You're in a dysfunctional relationship and it's never gonna work. Sorry!

If we could be true to ourselves, we wouldn't have to be so deceitful with other people. You know you really don't want to be in a relationship for real, so why lead a person on? If it's just sex you want, say that. Allow your partner to decide for himself/herself if they just want to be your sex toy. Don't decide for them; you have no right to make that decision for anyone. If all I wanted/needed was a sex

## DYSFUNCTIONAL

toy, I know exactly where to make a purchase with batteries. It's not rocket science, no strings are attached and no one's emotions are being played with.

We could be the best of friends if you're honest from the start, but don't make me develop ill feelings towards you because you're playing games....that wouldn't be good for you. People don't be so dysfunctional you don't know your worth. Others can only do what you allow them to do, and they will take whatever you give them. If you're doing all the duties of a wife/ husband without being married, you'll probably never be married....what's the point?

## CAN'T WE LEARN TO GET ALONG?

You know you're in a dysfunctional relationship, not only when the negatives far outweigh the positives, but the dynamics between you and the other person become irreversible; rather it be work place relationships, family relationships, friendships or what have you. It doesn't mean you're a bad person, just means relationships with certain people bring out the worse in you for whatever reason. Once you've gotten into dysfunctional habits with someone they become almost impossible to break. There are signs that you should recognize, signs that will tell you you're in a dysfunctional relationship.

## DYSFUNCTIONAL

If ever you find yourself having difficulties forming and maintaining intimate relationships, positive self esteem, trusting others and you fear losing control, you are dysfunctional. You have denied your own feelings and reality.

Functioning properly can easily be impaired by stressful circumstances, such as death, a parent's serious illness or differences in opinion and it happens everyday. It doesn't mean you take your frustrations out on other people... you learn to figure it out. Figure out why you're so envious and filled with so much hate. Figure out why you think no one will see you if you hide behind the make up.

## CAN'T WE LEARN TO GET ALONG?

Whatever it takes for you to live as close to normal as you possibly can, is what you should be focusing on. Not keeping up with the Jones' or walking around mad at the world because your friends wear Versace and you wear whatever's on sale at Family Dollar. None of that is important. What's really important is what you think of yourself.

Be able to look at yourself in that same mirror, not being disgusted and being able to see the inner beauty. Figure out how to let that person shine. If you can't be 100% real with yourself, then you're living a miserable life...

# DYSFUNCTIONAL

## That is so Dysfunctional!

You have to find that happy place within yourself in order to truly be happy with and for others. In all actuality, if you don't fix you, you will self destruct. People are going to live their lives in a manner that suits them. No one cares that you're living a fraudulent life, no one knows why you're so messed up inside or why you're so envious and filled with such hate. Therefore, you can't look for anyone else to help you. People only see the nice home you have, the good life you live, and the money you make. Some may pick up on how fake you carry yourself but they don't

## CAN'T WE LEARN TO GET ALONG?

know why and probably won't even care enough to ask.

No one, (other than family), knew I'd been abused, that was something that only I could deal with. I had to fix me. If you choose to walk around with your face balled up, mean mugging the world, then do just that but no one is gonna want to be around you...with your mad ass!

If you choose to grin in people's face, talking mad trash about them as soon as they walk away, have at it, word will get back to them quickly and you'll lose friends; one after the other. If you choose to throw a pity party for

## DYSFUNCTIONAL

yourself because you're unsuccessful, don't invite me, I'm not coming... I'll watch for the pictures on Facebook and comment on how simple you are. When you make it to the top and begin to look down at your friends, I will keep my distance because then you will have forgotten about all the roaches they helped you kill and the mouse traps they put down in your project apartment... Ijs. I will be that one friend to bring you right back down off your pedestal...try me! Remember how distant you were when you became the manager of McDonald's, couldn't tell you anything but when you got fired for stealing frozen chicken nuggets to feed your kids, you humbled yourself and had to ask for

## CAN'T WE LEARN TO GET ALONG?

forgiveness.... That ass needed everybody, and their mamas, lol!

You can pretty much tell that you're dysfunctional when you began to lie to people for no reason or lie to yourself then convince yourself that you're telling the truth. You make up stories in your head and assume everyone is talking about you, when you're not even relevant enough for a conversation. When you began to self sabotage because you're hell bent on self destruction. Even when things are good, you find every excuse to make things bad again...that's not just dysfunction, that's actually crazy as hell! You love drama, allowing the smallest things to

## DYSFUNCTIONAL

create it for you. Any little mishap or mis-communication, is opportunity for melodrama, who needs it?

You have to learn to compromise. People are so stuck on "my way or the highway" it's not even funny .Life is about compromise. Not everything is gonna go your way all the time (note to self). You have to be willing to do things, **within reason**, that you don't want to do, even if it's against your own plans. You can't leave issues unresolved, going to bed mad to avoid discussion or not working towards fixing your issues. Then you'll find yourself revisiting the same issues over and

## CAN'T WE LEARN TO GET ALONG?

over without resolution and nothing changes or gets better.

Now those of you who keep coming back for more might need to seek professional help; once you've found your way out of a bad relationship, why go back??? For some reason there is an attachment that breeds dysfunction. It's always easier to expect bad things to happen. I can only assume that it's less work to just accept all bad instead of working to make things good. You're always hurt, angry, but because you depend on drama and it's easier for you to deal with, you stay in that dysfunctional place.

## DYSFUNCTIONAL

Sometimes people have dysfunctional personalities. They can be caused by depression or anxiety. Being down all the time, that sense of misery, is very much on your mind. We all have heard the phrase "misery loves company". No one wants to be alone, and miserable, therefore, in order to have the company they long for, they stir up trouble in other people's lives, mainly the ones that are closest to them. It's not fair, but unfortunately, it happens. Either we can allow ourselves to sail with them on that misery boat to hell or choose to look the other way and be happy...you have to decide. Personally, I don't think I can entertain misery, not even for a second. It's too much

## CAN'T WE LEARN TO GET ALONG?

drama, requiring far too much attention and time... time that I don't have.

I've heard people say a listening ear will be blessed. I *may* listen to why you're so miserable but you better make it good, I will only hear it once. If I become bored with your sad story, I just might tune you out before you're done talking and get my blessings some other way. Anything or anyone I feel could possibly make my life more complicated than what it has to be, I stay away from. Life is challenging enough without all the drama. Why not just live and make the best of it?

## DYSFUNCTIONAL

If you're not willing to break away from dysfunctional relationships, rather it be with friends, family members, coworkers, significant others, spouses or what have you, you have to accept the fact that being dysfunctional is part of who they are. Don't expect them to ever respond in a positive way; it's not gonna happen. No matter what you say or do, they will only see things their way. Accept them for who they are, they'll never change... they don't see a need for change. Their behavior won't change, their way of thinking definitely won't change and the way they see the world will not change. You have to set boundaries around what you will and will not tolerate, and, stick to those boundaries. If not, you will find yourself giving in to their every demand and become just as dysfunctional as they are. How far you're willing to go and how much you're willing to put up with should determine if you want to continue on in the relationship. It won't get any better. Only when a person accepts that he or she is dysfunctional and desires to function properly, will they change and even then it could take months, possibly years to see a change. Their mindset has to change, an attitude adjustment will have to take place.

I'm no doctor, I can't be certain of this, but I don't think a person wants to be

## DYSFUNCTIONAL

dysfunctional.. I think something happened at some point in their life which caused them to become dysfunctional. Could be from having divorced parents, broken homes, being raised by single parents or society, who knows...could be from a number of things. Whatever the case, I doubt people wake up in the morning just deciding to malfunction. You cannot hate, or hate on people for no apparent reason, without there being some type of issue within. You can't think it's okay to be so jealous of people or be successful yet still be unhappy. Your confidence is at it's lowest low if you think you can't find a man or woman of your own. Your self esteem is

## CAN'T WE LEARN TO GET ALONG?

low as well if you stay with a person you know is cheating on you.

**Get it together people!**

Get yourselves together so you can function properly. It's not at all a crisis that you're in; try talking to someone you believe is functioning properly. There is hope for us all, at least I think so. I know that some people are just mean and it's not a malfunction, it's just who they are. They have some deep issues they may not be aware of, but we'll just pray for them....or whatever!

## DYSFUNCTIONAL

The entertainment world plays a major part in us all not functioning properly. We get so wrapped up in who is wearing what and how they're wearing it. Some even go broke trying to mimic what we see on TV, in the music videos, they actually forget what's really important. Women starve themselves to be thin like the supermodels in the magazines, having all types of plastic surgeries to look a certain way, silicone breasts..... It all goes back to not being true to who you really are.

**WHAT IS WRONG WITH THE REAL YOU?**

## CAN'T WE LEARN TO GET ALONG?

Why can't you accept the person God created you to be? You are exactly who *HE* wanted you to be so stop being selfish and ungrateful. It's one thing to enhance your natural beauty. Using a lil make up is one thing; I like the different color eye shadows, blushes, and even the eyelashes are okay when they don't cover your entire face, but when you start having surgery to look like what you see on TV, it says a lot about your character and how you really feel about YOU. The people you see on TV don't care anything about you, they're only marketing themselves to make money in order to pay their own bills. Same with the dancers you see in the videos, dancing is their way of life. The guys walking

## DYSFUNCTIONAL

around with their pants literally hanging off of their butts, some down to their knees, with their boxers showing, making it a fashion statement. The statement is "I'm dirty, my boxers are dirty, I may even stink and I have no respect for myself nor the people around me". Because you see some rappers dressed that way, you assume it's okay. It's not, it's dysfunctional, why not buy pants your size, and if they're still to big, put a belt on. That look is so unattractive and no one likes it for real.

Brothers, if you're over 25, lose the cornrows, it's not cute anymore. Just go see a barber, he/she will know what to do. I'm not in any

## CAN'T WE LEARN TO GET ALONG?

way, coming down on anybody at all, as I said before, I'm not perfect. I just don't get why we have to live in such a dysfunctional manner. Yes, I get that things happen in people's lives that may mess them up for a period of time, but it doesn't mean you have to stay messed up. We all have mishaps and shortcomings that make us uneasy with the lives we live, but we can't be consumed by those things. What's done is done! Move on, and be happy **deliberately**!

There is no real reason why we all shouldn't be able to get along. The next time you're alone, and in your mirror, be motivated to be the best you, you can possibly be. See the

## DYSFUNCTIONAL

beauty on the inside, not just the skin on the outside. Both men and women....men have self esteem issues just as women do.

Hug it out with your girls, or dap it up with your boys. Don't be so mad and ugly all the time; frowned up like everything around you smells bad. That's not cool! Bag all of your negativity up, leaving it for the garbage man, he'll handle it! Don't bring that foolishness around me, I'm just gonna laugh in your face! I'm not the one who pissed in your soup.

Seriously, you really should be mindful of your negative energy, it tends to put a damper on everybody's spirit. If you're down about

## CAN'T WE LEARN TO GET ALONG?

something, just stay away until you figure things out, your friends will understand and hopefully won't hold it against you. I've had quite a few dysfunctional people in my life; people on my job, people just passing through, and friends. All I can say is: Thank God for the ability to know when to move on. When things don't make sense to me or made sense at one time and I'm scratching my head about it now, I have to back away for a minute. When I began to question my own sanity, it's time to move on. Not everyone wants to function properly but as I've said earlier, you have to decide for yourself if you want to deal with dysfunctional people. I opted out and that works for me.

## DYSFUNCTIONAL

Yes, I would like for us all to be able to get along; our community, families, friends and all, but some just fall in the "pray for" category; those are the ones you stay away from. They don't recognize they are the ones bringing out the worse, the unpleasant personality that no one likes and they'll never change. The only change will be your surroundings, if you keep them around.

We all are dysfunctional as a whole because we don't try to work together or function properly as a union....you've heard it before, united we stand, divided we fall. It wouldn't be a quick fix but maybe an easy one if we simply came together. Now if you're just a

## CAN'T WE LEARN TO GET ALONG?

dysfunctional individual, it's deeper than trying to come together with anyone. Maybe there are some support groups in your area that can provide an objective perspective or individual counseling sessions. I guess you have to accept that you are dysfunctional, realizing dysfunctional is a problem. Sort of like being depressed, it puts a damper on your social life and it causes your relationships with other people to malfunction. Your relationship with your family, your friends, co workers, significant others, and spouses are all bad because you're dysfunctional. You should want to fix yourself; we all should fix ourselves so we all *can* learn to get along...don't settle for being

## DYSFUNCTIONAL

so **DYSFUNCTIONAL!!!!** This is your life, our lives, and it's too short not to live it to it's fullest potential, are you with me?

# ABOUT THE AUTHOR

Penelope D., born Penelope Yvonne Davis, was born and raised in Norfolk, Va. and currently resides there.

She wrote Dysfunctional because of all the hate and animosity she sees among us in society today...

"It scares me to think about what our future holds if we can't get it together now. Our kids, grand kids, and great grand kids will suffer. We need to get it together... Can't we learn to get along?"

**BOOKS BY PENELOPE D.:**
**My Strength Comes from Abuse**

# DYSFUNCTIONAL

# Author Penelope D.

## Research References
www.bustle.com
www.psychologytoday.com

www.ingramcontent.com/pod-product-compliance
Lightning Source LLC
Chambersburg PA
CBHW031422040426
42444CB00005B/679